T0070192

L X V E

A Heretic's Opium "Divine Intervention" —"an Interpretation"

Syncere

authorHOUSE®

AuthorHouse™
1663 Liberty Drive
Bloomington, IN 47403
www.authorhouse.com
Phone: 1 (800) 839-8640

© 2019 Syncere. All rights reserved.

No part of this book may be reproduced, stored in a retrieval system, or transmitted by any means without the written permission of the author.

Published by AuthorHouse 08/02/2019

ISBN: 978-1-5462-2238-5 (sc)
ISBN: 978-1-5462-2237-8 (e)

Library of Congress Control Number: 2017919414

Print information available on the last page.

Any people depicted in stock imagery provided by Thinkstock are models, and such images are being used for illustrative purposes only. Certain stock imagery © Thinkstock.

This book is printed on acid-free paper.

Because of the dynamic nature of the Internet, any web addresses or links contained in this book may have changed since publication and may no longer be valid. The views expressed in this work are solely those of the author and do not necessarily reflect the views of the publisher, and the publisher hereby disclaims any responsibility for them.

Under your tutelage
I've retained my youthfulness
Reclaimed
My usefulness...still, each useless step
Moments I've spent in contempt
every sigh of regret,
Every time
I cheated death, with each ready attempt
Is a tribute to you.
Love... (Agape)

Won't caption this
I am passionate
With the purging of fresh ink
From raw thoughts I couldn't ration with
Immaculate conception
Being mind fucked with no contraception
No contraceptive, impregnated pen
With genes, sixteens that bare my reflection
New nude thoughts that share my complexion
Black
And now the
world will react
Will I die in a genocide
By inhumane kind
With heroes that had a reason to ride?
Or will I come out alive?
I'm ready for the next time,
I walk plainly on Earth
Avenging the wrongs
I've encountered from birth

Young black male in
Society
I walk by a thin line
Quietly
Hardened
Strong
But where
Do I belong?

The draw of Haute Couture
Draping her contours
Leaves them
Coming at her door,
Ready to commit crime
For some time
With her alone
Physically to escape the tease all in their mind
She is a Jezebel
And she's sure to bring you hell
Under her spell
No man is safe, but pray tell
How is she adorned
With jewels like diamonds, gold, and sapphire?
Queen Babylon is a mystery to me
I watch her as she dances like midnight fire
The riches
For a good price
She will give you the time of your life
The spice of life
Like a gypsy
her lips be
Calling the aroused from
Below where her hips meet

I wonder sometimes
Some times I look at her
And imagine what she might look like
In another color
In another light
Could she ever be Mrs. Right?
Dark as
The night... but this is the life?
Seductive as hell
Why pray tell
Are you giving me
Hell?
Sin (fast life)

The gift of life
Shouldn't have to feel like a burden
But out here right now
There are real people who are hurting
Some fail to make
It back from slipping next to the crack
Adjacent to the vacant funneling
Parks where a few would hone their craft
Inner city stories we so poorly
Recognize on the map
Because this right here is America
It's as good as it gets when you're black.
My mind is as littered
As the ground covered with red tops
As busy as graffiti sprayed walls
Paying homage to our voice of hip hop
And the ever bustling struggle don't stop
Because I'm black
Should I walk around half dead
listening to a whole lot of nothing
Because I'm black, I mean it drowns
Out the bickering and the thumping
I mean the shooters know that
I'm black

Or brown depending on whatever light
You choose to see me in
Because I'm black should I
Walk around concealing weapons
Because I feel threatened
Because I'm black
Will I outlive diabetic comas
That tap me on the shoulder
Reminding me that I'm black and certain
conditions might arise as I get older
Is it inevitable to receive these sort of penalties
as a reminder that I'm black?
I know that I'm black
I realize that I have a story that no one
Else could tell...these tales aren't fiction
And because I am black, I will walk alone
To a throne to call my own
Just because I am black

Honing craft
My excellence is attributed to math
Acknowledging the pi within the graph
With enough fruit to feed a mass
They look and ask
While fallen angels callously laugh
Peeling off the mask
Of what so meticulously placed me back
At times the reformed I may retract
to measure the greenness of new grass
To track
progress, against what was given in the past
Are new horizons ahead?
Am I held back by what I dread?
I put the cancer stick to bed
I no longer feed my head
Voting out nonsense
To listen to the id behind
my already busy
mind
Tempted with the
pleasure principle

I realize that
I'm not invincible
My better judgement let's me know
I'm not invisible
Just
Miserable
Without therapy.

What do you do
When you've run out of options
And suicide isn't an option
Found inside good doctrine?
Wrestling with scripture you look up to God
But it seems as if he can't hear you
Try to escape trouble
Still the hustle of the snakes only draw near you
The world is a ghetto
And my man's got kids to feed
But if he dies young with no story to pass down
To his seeds, it will be my heart that grieves
In and out of prison
I listen to his wisdom
He got every reason to be mad at the world
Disenfranchised by the system
No psych wards
Can do him justice
Placebos can't fix your heart
Once it becomes corrupted
All I could give him is encouragement
A measly six dollars is all I had
Now I'm six dollars poorer
But I'm not even mad

We talk about freedom
Emphatically he would mention success
Our realities aren't one in the same
His back is stronger, it fuels the fire within his chest
Nonetheless... I confess
I got problems with my truth that I only know best
Under duress, and lack of sleep
Voices in my peace that done put me to the test
I got love for my brother
But what can I do?... except say a prayer
To the God
Upstairs whose hands has built the crystal stair
That Langston spoke of
With the tacks and boards all roughed up
Kind of like his world
Without love
So I extend my hand to him
Because he "Overstands" the man in him
And I can see
The man in him
Fighting his war without
His gun
In times like these, not only I am grateful about
The friends that we've become- Brother's Keeper

You are my drug
Withdrawal symptoms won't let me be
Serotonin won't bring me peace
Like the clanging on rickety old piano keys
I've sung this
song before
The lust for more
Rides me like a wave, but won't bring me to the shore
Drowning in dopamine
I look up to the sky
With my hand outstretched
Up high
Praying that God
Would have mercy on me
And set me
Free
As free as free verses
Swimming through my veins
All I do is
Complain
Within the empty thrill of normalcy
Are the hopes of growing sane
But I need it
Like the breaking of a new day

Pills replenish
Schizophrenics like the new craze
The fetish that left me
Un phased
what I think I really need
is a hit of this medicinal weed
To apply high grade first aid
Because I crumble underneath
With no peace
No release
On the illness
That has this hold on me – Drugs

Revolving doors
One shuts, and then I'm a fool
I stumble with no sobriety as if
A mixture of my elixir has been the fuel

That pulls to
Sets me back
God watches
I plan, he laughs-

Pauses... smirks heartily
With a knowing smile
And all the while
He knows I'm a wild child

I throw
Tantrums
Often times
Random

Constantly looking for answers
My way out of predicaments
I've mistakenly
Placed myself in-

At times I grin, so
Devilishly
When I think I'm right and lose it
When there is no therapy-

For a rapidly
Evolving mind
That mimics the
Grind...

Of door gears,
That move with my absence of fears
Then stub my toe
In front of sitting chairs

In front of an audience
That call out for sequels
To a storyline
That have yet to move people
To touch
The souls of men-
The need to
Fend

For
Our dreams
To end the struggle with all of
The baggage of self esteem-

I could do this
With no map,
I plan
God laughs-

When I was lost...

I would retrace steps.
Trying to...
Recover steps
Subdued...

To find directions...
Your smile and presence
Was my
Point of reference

As I came to realize...
Living life...
As my insecurities
Would soon come to a demise...

Morning sunrise...
In a zone like Weldon Irvine...
I'm drawn to tomorrow's surmise
Like an awakening for the wise...

A resurgence of an emerging... Reprise...
It's like the trance got me feeling some kind

Of way... In an unfamiliar state of mind...
A peculiar state of mind. Divine.

This groove got moods like
The hum of a baseline... The mood to a soundtrack I once knew...
Those days I swore by
And clung to...

Glory from ...under tough skin...
The epidermis... Beneath the surface... I'm deep blue...
Like the feeling behind my new view...
My ode to the zeal in forte the reason and the purpose, I paid dues...

Was loyal... But this bruise
Brought on fresh wounds.
Back to square one with no clue...
I was so true...

Now uninspired
By the few...
Wonders of this world...
That shine through...

There is none as
Beautiful like the smile I once knew...
In my limited
View...

Coveted like a
Fleet of vintage McLaren's...
Trying to make for
The once apparent...

Days of yesteryears... With no fear.
Trying to recollect pieces to a puzzle...
Cause they've
Been shuffled...

Drawn by the allure that brought on scenarios...
In a grandiose... theme of trouble...
That run through
Like life in the varicose veins of the struggle

I'm tired of not measuring up
To your specified quality, not a worthy recipient
But as your enemy...Etched on your throwing stones,
Imprints-

Of your "dreamt" up ideas
And preferences
Of an imaginary captured rebel soon to be made
The one built on hearsay and references-

You imagine me to be a nuisance
I was trouble in your eyes
But I stand as the scapegoat, and you seek
My demise-

It probably doesn't matter
How many times
I get struck with stones
Or how LOUD I may cry-

Out as I'm bombarded on trial
With the stones you chose to throw
I knew no refuge
I bowed my head low-

To duck and seek cover
I suffer
Like no
Other-

Because these are my wounds
And this is my time
I try to cover myself
I need my piece of mind-

Do away with my body
But my spirit will live
And soon the world will receive
The spirit and all of the cries I had to give- (Purpose)

Seldom is an artist free
Unless they're involved in a cipher
That's conducive to their art
Preaching to the choir "truth" to the inspired
Suiting for the fire
Wiping out the mire
Take a second look at life and it's processes
Objective perception that's in dire
Need to be translated,
Reciprocated
Appreciated
Elongated and propagated
Into new days, decades,
Centuries and millennia
Eons from years on
To incite new fire or calm brash hysteria
Ushered into the new age
While the scholars and sage
Turn the page
To the coming of age
To the dawning of day
Relay thoughts from souls that can't be bought
And new wisdom
That must be sought

I can't condone
Abandonment
Faint is the heart that beats for
Outstanding kids-

Justify
One could try
To rectify with the mind's eye, still
The blind leads the blind-

We live to die
Dwell in fire
To come out
Half alive...-

Half
Dead
With yesterday's issues
Still swimming through our heads...-

Stirs the soul...Heavy is the heart
That beats for stillborn
Neglecting the zombies we've become
Still torn from syndromes-

Just prone to attracting
The reenactment
Of unsightly
Lashings-

Sticks and
Stones
Can snap the spine
Like old wishbones.-

Rarely do we survive…
Unspoken lies
Affecting the next
Life… The hexed life.-

Some choose to live
In dishonor
Perpetuating
Trauma-

Harbored into
6 feet sleep, deep
Reincarnated from the womb,
Into the strolls of misery-

Going through
Deception, seldom
Do we stop in mirrors
To look at our reflection…-

Life is hard
So put up your guard
Guard your heart
We can finish before we start.-

Where r u God?

Mental note,
You can't play both sides of the field
That's if you plan to live long
Either you will take yourself out, or someone
will do u the favor, consider yourself warned
There are no level playing fields
Just mirages of conscious people
Stumbling with no symmetry
because among men there are no equals
Let no one define you
Put it all behind you
The past like ill-fated grass
As you risk it ALL to find YOU
The blind truth from divine roots
Observed with a sublime view
With no carbon copies
No times two
The scars are there to
Remind you
The past might be ghastly
But now It's time to re-design you
Far from the noise
And confusion
Far from the crew

And illusions
You owe yourself
An in depth conversation
You owe your mind's eye
Some new revelations
Grow, you can no longer utilize
Those slick alibi's
Some fools misinterpretation
As to why
You should hold onto the
Lies you used to hide behind
When you were too weak to appear
Vulnerable with the odds all in your mind
You need to win
By breaking the cycles
That left you so
Stifled.
And so... broken
So broken
So...
Open
Looking for a pillow
In a rose bed of thorns
Before
The dawn
Grew familiar to your
Shine
As the weight of the world
Put pressure on your spine...
Look for what you need
What you've needed the most
Eternal
sleep in a dose
Of reassuring words
That you've already made it
You can chill after the pill
Your time to rest is up for u to take it

We used to think sitting in confinement
Was a rite of passage
In spite of getting our
Ass kicked

By a justice system
That spews out victims as it does numbers
In the hundreds some want to bang, others to get fly
Escaping the trap of becoming

Just another number
Or a statistic
This is the life that we choose
To live with…

At times it feels as if…America isn't pure and White…
She's dark and sadistic
At times, my red blood in blue veins
Boils after bullshit

I've done witnessed
And as a casualty I am forced to live with
The terms love and equality as ploys and gimmicks

To attract my absence of thought I'm black
without a care as I diminish-

My right hand man
Caught a charge
But when he gets home
I'll make sure that he lives large

Yea we are going to be straight-
I battle with my mind daily
In the hopes to
Not grow crazy.

To make America great Again.
I feel we should revisit "Our Declarations of Independence."
Obscured in time,
Erased by the back of newer pens

Lady liberty
In the pursuit of happiness
Everybody wants to make a buck
In the pursuit of happiness

But when America
Has had enough of our cognitive dissonance
Lady liberty and her illegitimate
Children become as distant

Relatives
But is it all relative?
Perhaps, there is still hope
That we could give

And new life to be lived.

If I could paint a picture
In time
In inspired soliloquies
Outliving the harshness of these times

I'd speak victories
Into existence
Outlining true persistence
Commitment

Through verbatim and prove
I too, am brilliant
In
An instant

I live for days
Promised
And to be brutally
Honest.

I'd defy the harshness
And just speak
As I'd want to live,
And be who I hope to be

Sound in conviction... I was made for this
I was made to live
I got words to give...
So much hope to bring.

"Heaven" to disturb.
Imagine me ha! A young black kid...
If I could speak and impede upon any shred
Of doubt swimming through "nappy heads"

I would change
The course of time
For a time
With beautiful words that rhyme.

The addict,

Spatial inference
From a distance
My eyes glisten
From galactic wisdom-

Breaking down pyramids into isosceles triangles.
I relate. So much so that my new hypothesis bears weight
With the thoughts and philosophies
Of the greats...

Excerpts from a forgotten page
My curiosity enraged
I'm taken to Chapters rewritten by Langston Hughes
Stories that divides the few

Who strived in school
Kept alive by fools
Sanctioned by the
Likes of bigger fools...

With money and power
Placebos I take on the 9th hour

To put anxiety to bed
My sobriety needs to be fed.

I need peace in my life.
The addict.

Two alternate dimensions conjoined
by a common thread
like Siamese twins affixed by the points
one by the head-
undoubtedly, for you surely
had my mind
the other by the breast
with each beat suspended in time-
jazzy soulstress in the lime, rewinds
like inviting recliners in the mind
waiting for a chance with destiny...struck matchbox
roach clips, black soot trails like rain from the sky-
cigarettes and coffee
black with no milk,
no purity
no shame, no guilt-

Lust
And the drift
God looks down with a scope
that interrupts a stolen kiss-

A forbidden touch
I'm flushed and upset more than 20,000 miles
away from eternity, a sane mind
no i.d. tags for a lost child-

no identity-

Where is Venus?

What's wisdom
In the lips of a fool?
Except
A tool
To
Disarray
The buffoonery
That has caused me to go astray
Light a joint,
Smoke a L
To expel from the meaningless
Spell that I've become used to so well
Dwell in the last days
The last stage
Of venomous
Cancerous ways that has embittered my day
What's wisdom
In the lips of a fool
Except advice to momentarily escape the taste
Of the useless food that I've acquired at school
Our reality
Is that we become so accustomed to chasing salaries
To somehow fill the gap in our mentalities,
our existence in totality

But, whatever does
it mean
To even
Dream?
If I'm going to
Accept the things the way that they are,
yea, that job will
help me get that car
But that deal
Maaan, ... that deal
Will give me more
Appeal
To
Attract
A even larger
Bag
But what's wisdom in the lips of a fool?

You're a dream come true
Built like impeccable architecture
I've heard of sermons mentioning
Your name like vespers
You are the meaning of life
In ivy league lectures
Taught by masters who've known in measure
Who've felt the pressure
Of your presence in their lives
The beauty in Rhapsody
Intrigued I laid still motionless
As I dreamt in color, all too naturally
I've seen you, by way of supernatural waves
was in shackles, was enslaved
by the emptiness
of relentlessness drama that came my way
Back in my day
When life meant, that all we did was die
In the blink of an eye, we all
would come to drop like rain from the sky
Like the weight of reality
After the natural high subsides
The vacancy in complacency
No one to claim the kingdom inside

But my dream has revived
What was dead has come back to life
And now I realize
This is where my glory in song, in story resides
To which to all my failures confide
In the meaning of life
The revealing in time
The reason in plight
The reason I stride
And sing new songs
A dream come true
The rights for all the wrongs
I've seen, I've witnessed miracles
After relapsing from adapting
Reenactment of pain that clung
onto me with the strictest attachment
Like a casualty of tragedy, a raging masterpiece
Warring with myself over reasons to continue
Struck by the external, what seemed so eternal
Felt gentrified from inside the kingdom within u
As if I had no place
As if, I would know no rest
As if I couldn't do no wrong
As if it wasn't a test
Success, stress
Couldn't stand correct in the mess
There was
A disconnect
I couldn't hear, or wear
A ring, a call to a higher plane of existing,
The voice
Was so distant, I almost missed it
Persistent for commitment
On what level could I settle?
And escape the madness
That came from the devil

My time
has come
What's
done is done
Design
I've come to appreciate you like the texture
Cloth that covered me as I've dreamt
Of erect standing architecture, by your gesture
You've embraced my fall,
as I've nearly collapsed by your walls
And now I've awoke by your
Call...
Vienna

When expectations
Meets faith
You'll find yourself
In a different place..."
Alternative reality...
True art can't be compromised.
Just interpreted and
translated through beautiful lies
Segued into
The unfulfilled life.
Both gift and curse
Belong to none but the wise
The sleep are none
The wiser
Tossing and turning
Through the mire
Through the mire
Awakened just to grow tired
Of what used
To inspire.
Bastardized youth to
reach for the stars
And cling to crescent moons because the
pot at the end of the rainbow seems so far...

Away... Away.
After all any day might be the day
The soul is required
As the vessel begins to decay
True art can't be compromised
It's the summation of the being
The matrix
Of the being and the feeling
The experience in the seeing
The unraveling of believing
And disbelieving
To manifest in its season

How do you kill
something that you "love"
How do you throw away everything you ever wanted,
Everything that you ever dreamt of?

Your co-conspirators
Must've pushed u to the limit
Ego and pride
Prepared you for the finish

Chasing a fantasy
Drove you to insanity
Your fate promised you otherwise
Said it would all be beautiful...now tragically

You will atone... for this crime of passion,
you committed on your own
All
Alone

Where was your pride
When you cocked the load
Where was your ego when
You pulled the trigger with the ill intent to blow?

Now you're on your own
There's nowhere you could run
Sadly, now you recognize before your demise
Before the last note is sung

How do you kill something that you love?

Every time I
Pick up that pencil
I use it
As a utensil
To help cook up
Some food to help me eat
Because I am almost skinned n bones and I starve,
maybe some food will help me sleep
Every time I
pick up that pencil
I use it as a
Utensil
To forge some credentials
That will look good on paper
Because I'm nearly pushed away by society
I have no job plus a degree would look safer.
Every time I
Pick up that pencil
I use it as a
Utensil
To Help cook up
Some drugs to get high off of
Instant gratification sidelined against
blind fury looks more like blind love

Every time I
Pick up that pencil
I use it
As a utensil
To sketch out
Silhouettes of truth amongst a sect
Or a class of people to which there is no rival
Or equal but has not been paid their debt
I erase
I add
When I am hungry, healthy
Or sad
To illustrate what I know
To be true
Often times by
Silent hues
My time is due
To sketch out like the vibrant do
Alive is the fuse
That brings new information to the few
Shining through
The silver lining in the blues
That foster new
Aid to those blinded by propagandist views
Every time I
Pick up the pencil...I ask what will I draw next?
Will I write words
Or will I sketch?
At times, I scribble or draw between the lines
I ink up my flesh
Because tomorrow will be here
And yesterday has prepared me for death
But right now
I will draw
Like a fugitive
Against the law

What I leave
Might leave you in awe
The wise might say
I've seen something like this before
But, that doesn't concern me now
I'll just draw in this space of time
To bring peace
To my mind, and I will be fine
Just drawing

When you're riding high
You think you're there forever
However, no matter
How clever
You think you are to
Be understood.
Will the aftermath that you fall into
Serve you for a higher good?
Show-n-prove
Let the game do what it said it'll do
Let it school you
To the rules
The mechanics
For your enhancement
These are the prerequisites for the benefits
From the game you can take for granted
Planted seeds
Blossom in due time
The snare of the fowler rests
Under the break of every smooth line
A penny for my thoughts

Surface with purpose when it's due time
The wind blows and the melody is played
With every new chime
Same song is sung
Before you walk through the door
To see what's in
Store in the pursuit for more

The behemoth in me
Wants what's mine expediently
I'm under siege held in captivity by a beast
I need to succeed like I need to breathe...
Doubt just builds momentum as it creeps
And I just need to be free... Free
FREE to be
Free to believe, to release, to receive, to be relieved
So free to be... me
So I try to bargain with God, "if you agree to
Give me a zone I can call my own
I'll see to
It your name will be praised
Revered, remembered, and raised
From this empty existence I can only identify
As life, after all I am qualified by right, don't multiply my days
Quantified by phrase if it isn't vilified by your grace."
Vehemently my sorrow grows exceedingly
With meaningless days that are beneath me
I want what you promised to bequeath me
"Purpose, life and liberty." Still I hear you say to me
"I can only help if you will receive me
But you must believe me
I won't lighten the load just to make it easy

*I will enlighten you
It's only right to do
You will make
It through
I
Will do
just what I said
I will do."
Its been too hard living
And it's too long that I've been building
to just remain an outcast,
cast out like the villain*

Truth is (thinking)
I don't know if I'll ever fit in
It took me years to develop rather tough skin
Had to hide this light I had within
I took too many losses, striving to win
And after I let it all sink in, reminiscing
Temperature of this cold world was too frigid
The air was too thin
The chances of making it out was slim
Adjusting my eyes under a starry sky
Under my Yankees cap,
Navy with the wide brim, I reside in NY
My Genesis of adulterated sin
Striving for the win-win
Didn't feel like I belonged in circumstances
I was placed in, developed a heart under a tin
Shell... I ran with cowardly lions
And hair brained scarecrows
With too much pride
To let go
Disguised as guides to lead me
Out this land of Oz
Wanted to break through the sky,
knock on the door...sit and have a heart to heart with God,

Because I thought he couldn't hear me
Down where I walked, Lost as I was
Lost cause, with a need to floss
Just cause
Time would prove different, so I
Became more persistent, seeking wisdom
Had a few words to say to anyone who would
Listen, seeking love like new religion
Make it out of this algorithm,
with my own rendition from a vision, with precision
Come up from next to nothing
After executing winning decisions
I want to go
Beyond the other side of the rainbow
After collecting all that I could get
From this pot of gold, and let this world know
Take it from me,
if I make it you can make it
It takes a little time, a little patience,
A little hurt, but time is sacred
Don't mistake it
for what it isn't, listen
It takes courage, it takes strength,
It takes wisdom
It takes Love...
It takes words that will wake you
Up at 3 in the morning
Sleepless nights, Going out
for long walks up at the crack of dawning
It takes years of disbelief
It takes anger, it takes grief
It takes looking like you've lost your mind
In the middle of the street
It takes jogs
around the track
It takes talking to yourself,

It takes the audacity to laugh
Especially when the world
Wants to tell you no
"listen young heart
This ain't how it's supposed to go"
It takes years of being the underdog
And feeling that you don't belong
It takes time of doing right
Even when you know it's easier to do wrong
It takes putting the cart before the horse
Sometimes
It takes being oppressed
And being down and out all in your mind
It takes courage
to be yourself
To believe, when
Nobody else
Believes...
It takes planting
Seeds
Even when there is no applause
For your good deeds
It takes love
It takes love
It takes love
It takes becoming all that you dreamt of
In a
positive light
It takes overcoming death,
To walk into a new life
It takes being shot down
Numerous times
It takes haters laughing at slip ups
Hey man "remember the time?..."
It takes being made fun of
And people conspiring against you

It takes having the balls
To keep calm and letting God defend you
And maybe
just maybe....
It takes those losses to become everything
God said you would be,
Even though they thought you were crazy,
Yeah, maybe you don't have to fit in
Maybe you'll be OK just being different
Maybe you have to speak it
Into existence
Before you move,
Hey, what you got to lose?
Anyway... Anyway.
It takes love. (Agape)

Time...
Time is money
Either wasted, spent...earned
Ain't it funny
While it's used
Cordially
In pursuing life pursuits, time
Just moves accordingly
milliseconds gathers momentum
To the point, reality transforms
One soul dies
The other one is born
One hushed desire
Has seen it's lived out days in all of vanity
Eggs are hatched in the snap of reality
Talent meets a challenge confronting humanity
And I'm just drifting away
In the wonder of it all
Discover my voice
That almost brings me to my withdrawal,
Young but time moves
And seasons appear
Maybe this month
Maybe this year

I need to be compensated
As I speak into the universe
Give me some time
The reaper lurks
Soon to be balling
Out of control, these dividends
will make amends for time spent
Away from family and trusted friends
Earning
My stripes
While the clock just ticks
In the still of the night.

This is for the times
I couldn't sleep
The times
I felt too weak
To even speak,
The nightmares that troubled me
With visions of who
I was supposed to be
This is for every reason
To say no
The inhibitions
I just couldn't let go
The moments
In frustration that conjured up growth
The many times,
I had to wallow in the mud to and fro
This is for the day
I will smile a genuine smile
This is for the time I will realize
That the necessary pains were worthwhile
The manifestation
Of joy after delayed gratification
The day I will be greeted
in boardrooms with a befitting salutation

This is for my heart
This is for a brand new start
This is for the blessing from tragedies
This is for the lessons in art
This is for awakening to die
To bring forth a Renaissance
I'll sit in
The ambiance
On that great day and let it all
Sink in
And know, I won't have to
Face those days ever again. Amen. Grace.

Thought: it takes a wise person to know it takes a fool to become wise, and even in all of the madness there is order and discipline. Upon arriving to the next phase, you will fall sometimes but if God is directing you and guiding you through you'll eventually get to the next level. You've been through the bottom now see your way to the pinnacle of where you want to go. Wherever you're going. You might be out of bounds but you won't be out of reach as long as you keep your eyes on your prize. Guard your heart because what you desire if you're deserving you'll receive. Apply yourself and you'll succeed in any endeavor #grace

Printed in the United States
By Bookmasters